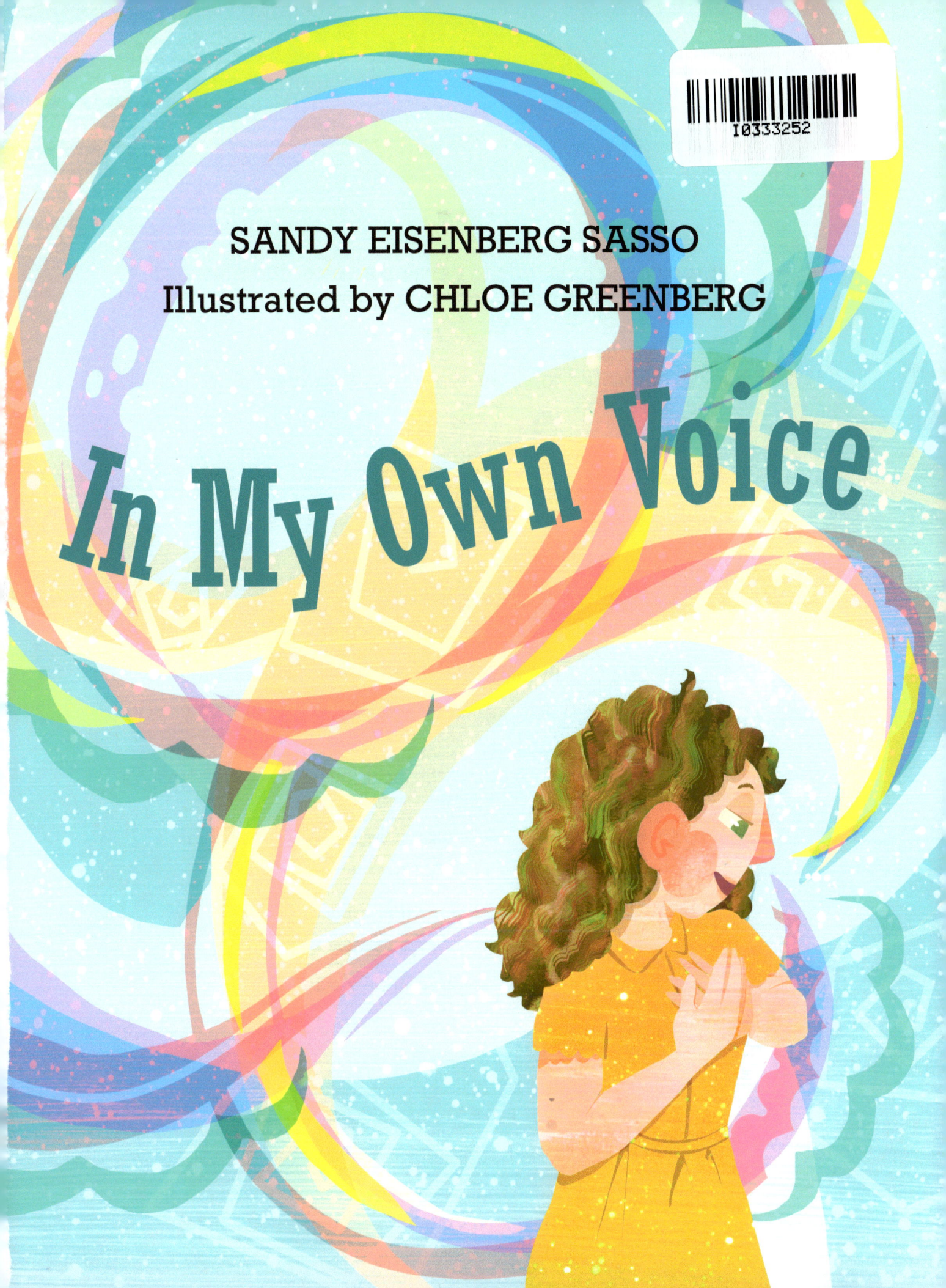

"It took me a long time to develop a voice, and now that I have it, I'm not going to be silent."
— Madeleine Albright

This book is dedicated to all the women who refuse to be silent.
— S.E.S.

Copyrighted Material

In My Own Voice

Text copyright © 2025 by Sandy Eisenberg Sasso

Illustrations copyright © 2025 by Chloe Greenberg

All Rights Reserved. No part of this publication may be reproduced, stored in a retrieval system or transmitted, in any form or by any means—electronic, mechanical, photocopying, recording, or otherwise—without prior written permission from the publisher, except for the inclusion of brief quotations in a review.

For information about this title, contact: IMOVbook@gmail.com

ISBN: 978-0-9980326-4-1 (Hardback)

ISBN: 978-0-9980326-5-8 (Paperback)

Printed in the United States of America

Library of Congress Control Number: 2024922703

"Listen," I call out to my mom at breakfast. "Today I finally start singing in my school choir. I can't wait."

I wish I had new patent-leather shoes, instead of ugly oxfords.

But I am not going to let anything ruin this day—not my shoes or the white ankle socks my mom insists that I wear.

Music is magic.

At school, I enter the choir room, adjust my eyeglasses, collect the sheets of music, and find my place. When the director gives the sign to begin singing, I open my mouth and sing with joy.

"**Loudmouth!**" the other students yell and put their hands over their ears. "You have a big mouth, just like your nose!"

I fight back tears.

"The boys sing just as loud," I grumble.

But no one seems to care.

But I do—in the synagogue, the one place where no one makes fun of me, where I feel at home.

One Friday night at Shabbat services, the cantor—who leads everyone in song and who sings deep from inside his soul—offers me a solo. "Yes!" I reply without hesitating.

So I keep singing,

year after year

Shabbat after Shabbat.

During one choir rehearsal, I say something out loud: "I want to be a cantor."

The cantor's eyes open wide, and his forehead wrinkles. "Barbara, you have a beautiful and strong voice, but you will never be a cantor."

"Why not?" I ask.

"Because you're a girl," the cantor explains.

"So?" I shrug my shoulders.

"Cantors are men!" he proclaims. "That is just the way it is."

I swallow hard and shake my head.

"I don't care. It's not fair.

I'm going to apply to cantorial school anyway!"

I tell my friends what I have decided.

"Are you sure?" they ask. "There has never been a woman cantor before. Ever!"

I reply, "I have to try." So I mail in my application.

I arrive at the cantorial school for my interview. My hands are sweating, and my heart is pounding. Three male cantors invite me into the classroom.

They are wearing shiny black suits and yarmulkas, the head coverings some men wear in the synagogue. They all just stare at me.

I worry.
Is my dress too short?
Are my shoes too clunky?
What about my hair?
Is there food on my face?
Why do they keep looking at me?

They ask me questions about myself. One cantor asks,
"Tell us, sweetheart—why really is it that you want to get into this school?
Don't you have any boyfriends?"

I wince, take a deep breath, and answer.
"I am not looking for dates, sir."

The cantors exchange glances and raise their eyebrows.
"You realize you would be the only girl in the school?
You might not even get a job."

Finally, the cantors ask me to perform.
When I start singing, all my nervousness disappears.
I love making music.
To my relief, I see that now the cantors are smiling.
I relax.

Eventually, they shake my hand and say, "Thank you for coming. You will receive a letter with our decision."

After a few weeks, the letter arrives.
My hands shake and I open it.

I gasp and shout to the empty room,

"I'VE BEEN ACCEPTED. I AM GOING TO BE A CANTOR!"

I take two buses through the rainy streets of New York to get to the school. When I arrive, my coat is drenched and my hair is sopping wet. I tug at the heavy double doors to enter the building.

The halls smell musty, like old books and steam heat,
and the brass doorknobs need polishing.
I don't care. This is where I want to be.

The class I am most excited about is Chorus.
But when the director sees me, he frowns.

"I don't have a part for you—only for men's voices.
I guess you will just have to mouth the words."

The other teachers don't mind if I sing.
But they want me to sing like a man.

How am I to do that?

When I sing low, people say, "We can't hear you."

When I sing high, they say,
"You are too shrill. No one will be able to sing with you."

I make a decision: I will speak and sing like the men.
I will lower my voice, so that it sounds powerful.
But then people say, "You're bossy."

One kind teacher advises me, "Barbara, use your own voice."
I ask, "But what if it's wrong? What if no one wants to listen?"
He just shakes his head and says, "Let your soul sing."

"I remember my childhood cantor," I tell him. "He sang from his soul.
His voice was firm, strong, and holy.
I know all the right words and notes, but I'm afraid."

"Barbara," he exclaims, "Let YOUR voice come out."

This time, I sing from deep inside my soul!

"That's it!" he cheers.

I am a cantor.

I teach.

I read Torah.

Dear Readers,

I wonder if anyone has ever made fun of your hair, your dress, or the way you talk or sing?

Are you ever afraid to speak up because you think people will make fun of you?

Who gives you courage to keep trying to do something, even when it is unpopular?

I wonder if there is something you like to do as much as Barbara loved singing?

Request for Reviews:

I really hope you enjoyed this book! If you did, I'd be very grateful if you would take a moment to leave a review on whatever site you prefer.

Thank you very much!

—*Sandy Sasso*

The cantorial tradition is almost two thousand years old. It arose from the role of the Levitical priests, who sang psalms in the Great Temple in Jerusalem. Until recently, women were not allowed to lead the community in prayer. When the first schools for cantors were established, only men were admitted.

Cantor Barbara J. Ostfeld, the first ordained female cantor, was admitted to the Hebrew Union College-Jewish Institute of Religion School of Sacred Music (now called the Debbie Friedman School of Sacred Music) in 1970, and she was ordained in June of 1975. Many more women followed her into the cantorial program, beginning the very next year after her admission. There are now at least eight cantorial schools that accept women, and today there are many hundreds of female-identifying cantors around the world.

Cantor Ostfeld served for twenty-seven years as cantor of congregations in Clifton, New Jersey, and in Great Neck, Rochester, and Buffalo, New York. She then served for ten more years as the placement director of the American Conference of Cantors. Cantor Ostfeld retired in 2012. Her memoir is *Catbird: The Ballad of Barbi Prim.*

About the Author

Rabbi Sandy Eisenberg Sasso is the author of *The Shema in the Mezuzah* (National Jewish Book Award), and *Regina Persisted: An Untold Story,* as well as of *Judy Led the Way, God's Paintbrush, Sally Opened Doors,* and many other children's books. Her latest books are *I Am Not Afraid: Psalm 23 for Bedtime* and *Miriam's Dancing Shoes.* She is Senior Rabbi Emerita at Congregation Beth-El Zedeck in Indianapolis, founder of the Religion, Spirituality, and the Arts Initiative at Indiana University at Indianapolis, Herron School of Art and Design, and cofounder of Women4Change Indiana. She lives in Indianapolis.

About the Illustrator

Chloe Greenberg is a book illustrator and collage artist, based in Cincinnati. After her college career at Herron School of Art and Design, she became the illustrator of author Kati Hirschy's *My Autistic Mama,* a children's book that presents a positive image of autistic traits. Chloe's illustrations draw inspiration from her background as a musician and songwriter, and aim to visually represent music with expressive textures, intentional colors, and flowing compositions.

When she isn't making art, you may find Chloe birdwatching at her local park, going to concerts with friends, or watching movies.

www.ingramcontent.com/pod-product-compliance
Lightning Source LLC
Chambersburg PA
CBHW041436010526
44118CB00002B/88